365 Days of Motivation

A Guide to Success in Life & Business

Tammy L. Turner

Copyright © 2013 by Tammy L.Turner

This edition published in 2013 by Kapstone Publishing

Compiled and edited by So It Is Written, LLC

All rights reserved. No portion of this publication may be reproduced without the prior written permission of the publisher.

Cover Design: Ivory Coast Media

Photograph for Cover Design: Wayne Norman Photography

Typesetting: Stephanie Lewis, 23 Exchange LLC

ISBN: 978-0-615-73610-5

www.mytammyturner.com

Printed and bound in United States

DEDICATION

To my loving husband, Lance:
I am because we are! I love you more than mere words could ever articulate. You are everything that I have ever dreamed of and more than I imagined. Thank you for loving and supporting me.

To my niece, Taylor Renee Turner:
Auntie loves and misses you.

WHAT IS MOTIVATION?

mo•ti•va•tion

noun \ˌmō-tə-ˈvā-shən\

Definition of MOTIVATION

1

a: the act or process of motivating

b: the condition of being motivated

2

: a motivating force, stimulus, or influence : INCENTIVE, DRIVE

First Known Use of MOTIVATION

1873

Related to MOTIVATION

Synonyms: boost, encouragement, goad, impetus, incentive, incitation, incitement, instigation, momentum, impulse, provocation, spur, stimulant, stimulus, yeast

PREFACE

This book, *365 Days of Motivation*, took four years to complete. In the midst of the madness or chaos, better known as our everyday lives, it's difficult to stay motivated. I read a variety of inspirational quotes, posts from inspiring people on Facebook, and even reflect often on words of wisdom that my mom passed along to my brother and me as children.

It's difficult to be motivated, focused and encouraged when you're hungry or don't have shoes on your feet. It's difficult for you to stay mentally stimulated when your surroundings and circumstances encourage the exact opposite, but that's when it's most important to stay motivated. Years ago, I realized I had (and continue to have) a passion for helping people. I help by listening; I help by encouraging; I help by inspiring; I help by motivating. During the four years of my writing journey, a little tool known as Facebook helped me capture, document and archive all of those motivational notes that I once only shared with my friends. This book is a compilation of four years of motivational notes designed to encourage the reader to be happy, to be focused, to purse your dreams, to help others pursue their dreams and to avoid negativity and others who think negatively.

This is not to be used as an ordinary book. It is not to be read in chronological order. Don't start at the first page, which is January 1st. Start with your birthday. My birthday is July 12. So if I'm reading this book for the first time, that's the day that I will skip to first. After you read the words of inspiration on your birthday, skip next to your spouse's or significant other's birthday. Read those words and then share them with him/her.

Next, skip to the dates of your children or your siblings. Share those encouraging words with them (depending on the age of your children, you may need to ad lib). Now that you have identified some words of motivation for yourself and your loved ones, let's go to where we are today. Let's go to today's date (the date you began reading *365 Days of Motivation*). We'll take this journey together.

In the midst of everything that is going on in our world today, we all need to stay inspired, encouraged, focused and motivated. We will stumble a lot on our way up or on our way down. *365 Days of Motivation* helps you deal with those stumbling blocks and turn them into stepping stones by helping you become more proactive versus reactive. My words over the course of those four years didn't only serve to motivate my audience, but my words were also a reminder to me to stay focused and stay the course.

Those that have followed my journey on Facebook, knew (and expected) that I would end all of my daily quotes with the words, "Let's Go!", which is symbolic to my audience to let them know we are in this together.

In an effort to make this piece as authentic as it has been over the course of four years it was written, I have added "Let's Go!" at the top of each page instead of at the end of each quote. As you read your daily words of inspiration, don't forget to add a "Let's Go!" after you recite them.

May the words on these pages assist you in blossoming in to whom and where you want to be.

Cheers,
Tammy

JANUARY

January 1st

What are you willing to give up to realize your dream? Are you willing to give up TV time, sleep, socializing on the weekends with friends or time spent on Facebook? Decide what you are willing to sacrifice to make your dream come true...then execute!

January 2nd

Don't allow distractions to make you lose focus of your goals. Distractions will come in many forms: work, family, friends, and even depression. Recognize it for what it is: a distraction! Stay focused and stay the course. You got this!

January 3rd

Everyone at some point in their lifetime should know what it's like to truly experience unconditional love. I'm not speaking of the love from a parent to a child. I'm speaking of love experienced between two adults. I can honestly say, for the first time in my life that I have experienced unconditional love and have been on the receiving and giving end of it. It's a beautiful thing, truly a blessing.

January 4th

We can choose our friends, but we can't choose our family. Wisdom has taught me that *family* doesn't mean those who celebrate your successes and support and encourage you through your failures. Sometimes family means, "I love you and I'll see you at the reunion." Everyone, *family* or not, won't share your vision. Don't let them kill it either. Protect your dreams!

January 5th

If you seek to grow in your business, your profession or your personal life, take a look at what you need to change to make that growth possible. Maybe you need to make a little extra effort, or spend a little extra time. Push yourself out of your comfort zone. Growth is impossible without change. Get started today!

January 6th

Can you see beauty, even if it's not pretty every day? Ladies, if a man can see you at your worse (physically, spiritually and emotionally) and still see how beautiful you are (inner and outer beauty), you've got a winner! Gentlemen, it's important for you to let your lady know that she is beautiful!

January 7th

I love my life, my businesses, my friends, my husband, my family, my in-laws, and myself. I am happy in my skin and excited about my future. What about you?

January 8th

Team Maddox has been making moves. What a blessing it is for the person you love to be your partner, your balance, your inspiration, your cheerleader, your rock, your guide, your listening ear and your best friend. I never knew it was possible to love another person (that I didn't give birth to) this much. Feeling *loved* and *empowered*. Hope you are too!

January 9th

I'm not that special. Not at all. I put my pants on one leg at a time just like everyone else. What's different about me? My thinking! I truly believe I have *no* limitations. Because I believe that I can do any and every thing that my heart desires, the world is my playground. I *can't* stop and I *won't* stop!!

January 10th

Be leery of 'fair-weather' friends. You know those people that are around *only* when the good times roll. Surround yourself with people that will stick and stay, support and encourage you even if they don't fully understand what you're going through. Seek friends that can weather the storm.

January 11th

You are significant! *Your* presence is important to someone. *Your* touch is needed by someone. *Your* love is returned by someone. *Your* voice is music to someone's ears. *Your* laugh is a melody to someone's heart. Take the time to get to know who you are! You are appreciated!

January 12th

Be passionate about what you do and grateful for what you have, instead of envious of what someone else is doing and what they have. You can't walk in *your* purpose, worrying about what someone else is doing.

January 13th

A year from now, you will wish you had started today. Don't let this become your story. Do it today. Start that venture or project now. Begin with the end in mind. Always remember that "procrastination is the enemy of progress." You can do it!

January 14th

Every day presents a new set of challenges. Every day presents a new set of obstacles. The key to all of them is your perception. Take the optimistic approach and view those challenges as opportunities. View those obstacles as possibilities. Your perception is the key!

January 15th

Look again! Those blocks you tripped over were not stumbling blocks at all; they were actually building blocks and stepping stones. You stumbled so God could get your attention and redirect your focus, effort and energy. So use those blocks to build.

January 16th

I am looking forward to the most *amazing* day! I expect happiness, focus, love, laughter, fun and encouragement to *dominate* my day, and I welcome their presence. Bring it on!

January 17th

In line with the 'Occupy' movement, let's occupy our minds with positivity; occupy our hearts with kindness and love for one another; occupy our communities by being good neighbors; occupy our relationships by being unselfish; occupy our schools by becoming mentors; occupy our future by lifting as we climb! What are you occupying today?

January 18th

It's a beautiful thing to be able to look at the man you love and still feel the same butterflies, the same attraction, and the same magnetism that you felt when you first met. Actually, time and love has heightened the experience. But I still get that same feeling I got the first time I laid eyes on him. Twenty years from now, I still want to feel that same way.

January 19th

Today, focus on being creative; on being bold, on being courageous, on being a resource to others, on being kind, on being loving, on your goals, on your dreams, on helping someone else realize their dreams. I know that's a lot to focus on for one day but I know you have the ability to multi-task. I believe in you!

January 20th

When you feel good about yourself and your direction, and you *know* your purpose, you can move mountains! I see mountains turning into mole hills as we speak!

January 21st

Never accept mediocrity! It's not an option. Be the best. Give your best and only accept the best!

January 22nd

Never make someone a priority in your life when you're simply an option in theirs. You get what you settle for.

January 23rd

Family, sometimes we are so focused on distractions (problems, relationships, finances, etc.) that we take our focus off of our goals. Anything that pulls you from your goals and dreams are distractions. We all have curve balls thrown at us, but don't get "stuck dodging balls" and being thrown off of your square, and lose sight of your goals or dreams. Stay focused, stay the course.

January 24th

I woke up this morning and opened my eyes to my future. I inhaled determination and focus into my lungs. When I got out of bed to stretch, I found myself reaching for the stars. I prepared myself a healthy breakfast complete with motivation, affirmations, inspiration and a healthy dose of faith. I started this day and every day with a P.M.A (Positive Mental Attitude). I hope you will choose to do so too!

January 25th

No matter what you go through, how many disappointments you have, what obstacles you encounter or the number of times you fall down, don't give up. Don't quit. Don't ever stop fighting. Keep pushing forward.

January 26th

Family (and I say this very affectionately) please, please, PLEASE stop taking pictures in the bathroom mirror and posting them on Facebook! Consider how you are damaging your personal brand. *This has been a public service announcement.*

January 27th

Sometimes we can be our own worst enemy. We live in the past and beat ourselves up with feelings of guilt and regret over past mistakes, and we stifle ourselves with negative thinking. We have to learn to love ourselves, forgive ourselves, and change our thinking. Get the lessons from past failures and use them to grow. You got this!

Let's Go

January 28th

I'm on absolute *fire* today! I'm excited about my future, excited about the possibilities, encouraged, inspired, focused and determined. I believe that I can do anything and everything that I set my mind to. So, I'm strapping on my seat belt, pressing the gas and getting ready for a glorious ride. Who's with me?

January 29th

Inspiration can come in many forms and shapes. I'm inspired by birds chirping outside of my window because I can see God in them. I'm inspired by watching children play because I know they have not yet been tainted by the disappointments of the world. I'm inspired by breathing air into my lungs because I know I still have a chance to pursue my dreams and help others pursue theirs. There's inspiration in everything you do and see. Find it!

January 30th

Smile and be happy today. Don't let the world, your job, the traffic, other people, your circumstance, or negativity steal your joy. Make a decision to be happy, no matter what. Your attitude will determine your outcome!

January 31ˢᵗ

There are those that *make* it happen, those that *watch* what happens and those that *wonder* what happened. Join the movement of doers and *make* it happen! ~

Let's Go

FEBRUARY

February 1st

If you continue to give up, quit or make excuses, you will never reach the finish line. Press harder, find ways over, under, around or through your obstacles. Stay focused, stay the course.

February 2nd

When is the last time you experienced a random act of kindness? Do you remember how good it made you feel? Help someone feel that today. Do something for someone out of the kindness of your heart without expecting something in return.

February 3rd

I woke up this morning feeling abundantly blessed and loved! What a great feeling! Boy, I tell ya, love is an energizer, a motivator, a get-ya-thru the rough patches and curve balls that life throws you. It inspires, it uplifts, it encourages, it strengthens, it guides and it provides a sense of peace in a sometimes crazy world. Yes, love is beautiful. But remember that it starts with *self*. Let's spread some love today!

February 4th

Naysayers and dream-stealers BEWARE! Your opinions are not wanted, welcomed or needed. I choose to surround myself with motivated, positive, goal-oriented people. If you're able to read this, you are obviously in the second group.

February 5th

The difference between *possible* and *impossible* is your thinking! If you believe you can't, you won't. It's just that simple. If you *believe* you can, you will find a way or make a way. The choice is yours. Believe in yourself!

February 6th

Some days we fall off our square and some days we get knocked off our square. No matter how you got off your square, get yourself back on track! Regain your focus, learn the lesson and get back in the game. Plan, prepare and execute!

February 7th

Strength doesn't always equate to muscle mass. Sometimes strength is quiet; sometimes strength is patient; sometimes strength is exhibited by love; sometimes strength is exhibited through friendship; and sometimes strength is a simple apology. Sometimes strength is learning when and how to say, "No." Be strong today.

February 8th

The five P's: Proper Preparation Prevents Poor Performance! ~ Are you prepared? Are you prepared for life, for love, for success, for that new job, even for happiness? If the answer to any of these questions is, "No," what steps are you taking to become adequately prepared? Don't be surprised. Be prepared! Don't blame others. Be prepared! Challenge your excuses!

February 9th

Before you can love your neighbor, your spouse, your children or anyone else, you must first learn how to love yourself. We love many things and many people, but we neglect our own minds, our own spirits, and our own bodies. Let's show ourselves some love today by investing time into something that will make us better, stronger, wiser and more spiritually filled.

February 10th

Today, get to the root of what's holding you back. Get to the root of what is causing you fear in your business, career, relationship or family. Get to the root of what that is and then pluck it out! Let nothing stand in the way of your progress. Sometimes it's our own pride that needs to be plucked out. Whatever it is, let's get rid of it today and get back to the business of being productive.

February 11th

Today, examine the habits that you have formed. Do they yield good results or do they keep you stagnate? Discipline yourself enough to begin to break those bad habits and replace them with habits that yield positive results in your life.

February 12th

Stop complaining! There is *power* in your words! Your words and thoughts attract either negativity or positivity. If you want success, speak it into existence. If you want happiness, speak it into existence. If you want peace, speak it into existence.

February 13th

Today, let the people who support you (through the good times and bad) know that you love and appreciate them. People are always around when the good times roll, but when have true friends that help you through the rough patches, celebrate them.

February 14th

Back in the day when folks stabbed you in the back, they did it while you weren't looking. Nowadays, they do it under the guise of friendship and look you in the eye while sticking the knife in your side. Here's my answer to that: No weapon formed against me shall prosper! ~ You cannot and will not stop my stride! What God has deposited in me is more powerful than the mischief or maliciousness that you carry in your heart.

February 15th

Leaders lead by example. Leaders don't gossip and create tension and unrest amongst the individuals that support them in their roles. Note: If you're a leader and no one is following you, you're not leading; you're just taking a walk.

February 16th

What doesn't break you only serves to make you stronger. I thank God today for giving me strength instead of bandages. I thank God for the ability to forgive those that tried to break me and for the friendships that made me stronger.

February 17th

I'm celebrating *you* today! Give yourself a pat on the back. You are a champion! You have persevered when you were discouraged. You pressed harder when it was easier to give up. You are fulfilling your dreams and helping others fulfill theirs. You are leading by example. You looked fear square in the eye and said, "Not today." Good job! It's alright to give yourself a high five from time to time; just remember to stay humble.

February 18th

Don't allow someone's opinion of you to become your reality.

February 19th

Stop taking advice from people that are not qualified! An accountant cannot tell a surgeon how to perform open heart surgery, nor can someone that has no children tell me the best way to raise mine. Take advice from people that have traveled the road that you are on. Even though their advice may not be the best, at least they've been down that road. We take advice about our lives, love, dreams and business from people that have made poor choices in their lives or love and never pursued their dreams or business aspirations. Stop that.

February 20th

Today let someone know that you believe in them. Let them know that they can fulfill their dreams. Let them know that you support them. Let them know that you will help them get there. Let them know they are not alone.

February 21st

Rejection is God's protection. Don't get stuck in the past, thinking about what coulda, woulda, shoulda. Focus on the future. But don't forget to live in the moment. God closes some doors so you can appreciate the beautiful view from the window.

February 22nd

I woke up *hungry* this morning. I had some faith and vision for breakfast with a side order of determination. I washed that down with a full plate of focus, a dollop of passion, and of course B12 and courage vitamins. This is the breakfast of champions.

February 23rd

You are the architect of your house and your destiny! Whether a house or a pyramid, the blueprint lies within. Dream, plan, build! Then, repeat!

February 24th

Procrastination is the enemy of progress! Let's get in the game *today*. Figure it out, talk it out, play it out. Do whatever you need to do. Just get in the game.

February 25th

You got it! You already have everything you *need* to be all that you *want*. You are able, you are intelligent, you are blessed, you have faith, you have courage and you have determination. Now what are you going to do with it?

February 26th

I want to give a shout out to single moms. You deserve recognition and should be applauded. My mom was a single mom. My dad offered no support during my upbringing. It's unfortunate, but I'm not stuck there. My mom didn't make all the right choices, but she did the best she could with what she had and I appreciate her for that. She could have given up, like my dad, but she didn't. Single moms, we see you and appreciate all you do to make sure your children excel! Stay encouraged.

February 27th

You never know what storm a person is going through. You never know what trials and tribulations they've just overcome. We oftentimes are so quick to judge people, but couldn't walk a mile in their shoes. Let's practice kindness, love, patience and forgiveness with people. Your kind act or gesture could make the difference in their life.

February 28th

I choose to see the best in people. I choose to see God in people. I don't look for people's faults, shortcomings, or what they have or don't have. We all have shortcomings, but we all have God in us as well. So stop talking about folks and instead learn to see God in them.

February 29th

Facebook has made changes. Go with it. The world is constantly changing. Either you adapt or you get left behind. Get out of your comfort zone.

MARCH

March 1st

Stretch yourself today! Stretch your imagination, your comfort zone, your possibilities; you're thinking, your patience, your love, your life. Challenge your excuses and let's make it happen!

March 2nd

Your *attitude* will determine your *altitude*! If you approach life, success, happiness, love, challenges, or business with a winning attitude, you will always come out on top! You have the ability to decide whether your attitude will help you or hurt you. The choice is yours. I choose to win. I choose to soar. I choose to be infectious. Therefore, I have a winning attitude. What about you? ~

March 3rd

I choose not to participate in the recession. I choose to create opportunities for myself and my family. I choose to be successful. I choose to prosper and help those around me prosper. I choose to press harder. I choose to make the extra effort. I choose to go the extra mile. I choose to make it happen because I choose not to lose. Join me.

March 4th

Love heals. It rejuvenates, excites, and ignites. LOVE trusts. It hides all flaws. LOVE compromises, supports and strengthens. Love lets you know you don't always have to be right. I'm so glad that I know love.

March 5th

I want you to get uncomfortable today! Introduce yourself to two perfect strangers (networking); make that phone call you've been putting off; forgive that person that angered you; set 3-, 6-, and 12-month goals for yourself; tell your spouse that you appreciate them; let your children know that you appreciate the love and laughter they have brought into your life; show someone a random act of kindness.

March 6th

I'm traveling with my buddies today: focus and determination. We're going to pick up courage and faith along the way. Once the four of us get together, we're going to brainstorm and develop a strategy to achieve our goals. We've made a pact to be each other's accountability partner. With buddies like these, I can't go wrong! Hope to see you along the way.

March 7th

Success will not walk down the street one day and simply just jump in your lap. Nor will it fall from the sky. Nor will someone build your dream for you, then deliver it to you gift wrapped. *You* have to build your dream; *you* have to grind; *you* have to make it happen.

March 8th

I'm exercising my rights today—my right to be happy; my right to turn a frown into a smile; my right to be a blessing to others; my right to be blessed by others; my right to motivate and inspire; my right to lift as I climb! Exercise your rights today!

March 9th

When folks attempt to knock you off your square, simply stand firm! Plant your feet, look them in the eye, and repeat after me: "Not today!"

March 10th

Don't forget to be thankful and give praise to God when things are good and you are being blessed. Sometimes our only conversation with God is when we are going through troubling times or in need. Talk to God when you just want to say, "Thanks for blessing me; thanks for providing for me; thanks for covering me; thanks for guiding me; thanks for allowing me to open my eyes today. THANK YOU!"

March 11th

Are you a fire-*lighter* or a fire-*fighter*? Today, be the spark that ignites someone's soul on fire! I'm planning to be an inferno today; what about you?

March 12th

Change your thinking. Let's get it going today! I'm thinking how much I can get done today; how I can maximize tomorrow and how can I knock it out of the park the next three days after that. Maximize your opportunities today.

March 13th

You are a walking, talking testimony to God's greatness. Reflect on the things that God has brought you through, and those things that made you better, stronger and wiser. Sometimes people lose faith and they may need to hear an encouraging word from you. Share your testimony and help others stay encouraged and focused.

March 14th

Today, I visualized myself being and doing exactly what I wanted to accomplish. I visualized all obstacles being removed from my path. I visualized myself being surrounded by people with the same positive energy that I have and we are encouraging each other. I made a choice to be successful. I made a choice to be happy. I made a choice to change lives. I hope you have too!

March 15th

Don't declare bankruptcy on your dreams! As long as you can conceive it, you can make it happen! I don't care how many times you fall down or you've been knocked down. Quitting is *not* an option! You have too much to do. You have lives to touch and people to bless with your gift.

Those obstacles make you stronger; use them as stepping stones to get to the next level.

March 16th

You don't have permission to tell me, "You can't." You don't have permission to tell me, "Your dreams are too big." You don't have permission to tell me, "You should wait." You don't have permission to tell me, "That's not realistic." You don't have permission to extinguish my dreams--and until I give you permission (which will be the 33rd of never), keep your opinions to yourself because I don't want them.

March 17th

I don't know how to quit; nor do I want to learn!

March 18th

We ask for wisdom, but we do things that are not wise. We ask for guidance, but we try to lead our own way. We ask for love, but we do and say things that are not loving. We ask for patience, but don't exhibit it when dealing with friends, family, business associates and loved ones. We ask for help, but we're unwilling to be a resource to others. My point is that we need to be that which we ask for.

March 19th

All I ask this day is that God uses me as a vessel through my thoughts, my speech and my deeds. Think through me. Act through me. Move through me that I, in some way, may be a blessing to others.

March 20th

Today, let's practice love. Let's exercise patience. Let's give our best and be our best. On your journey today, you will encounter obstacles; refuse to be distracted. Stay focused and stay the course.

March 21st

Will not stop. Will not quit. Will not give up. Will press harder. Will become stronger. Will help others. Will grow. Will stretch. Will lift. Will not be deterred. Will not be distracted. Will live and walk and breathe--*my* purpose, *on* purpose.

March 22nd

Unbelievable! I saw a fight this morning. I saw courage put fear in a headlock. I saw optimism put a choke hold on negativity. I started to jump in and break it up, but I looked up and success *and* determination intervened and it looked like they had the situation under control.

March 23rd

I realize that I'm allergic to drama and negative people. So, to make sure I'm fully vaccinated, I inject myself with a daily dose of love, positivity, happiness, faith, courage, determination, strength and vision. I'm developing immunity to all negativity and I'm walking in my purpose!

March 24th

Just when you think it can't get any better, it does! I'm claiming abundance, happiness and prosperity today! Yep, it's mine! But there's enough for all of us! Come get a piece of the pie.

March 25th

As I navigate through this thing called life, I am reminded that sometimes the water is choppy, the current is strong, my sail may not hold up and a storm is coming. But rest assured; I've got my life jacket on and when given the option of sink or swim, I'm gonna swim! Whether it's the backstroke, breaststroke, freestyle or the butterfly, I will get to the other side. I may be tired when I arrive, but sinking is not an option!

March 26th

Today, take a look in the mirror and tell the person you see, "I believe in you! I have faith in you! I hear you. I see you. I know you. I respect you. I love you." Let's practice loving ourselves and therefore being able to love others.

March 27th

As long as you continue to do what you've always done, you will continue to get what you've always gotten. If you don't like what you've received in the past, make a conscious decision to do things differently. Make a change and your results will change.

March 28th

As children, we often heard the words, "On your mark, get ready, set…go!" We took off running at top speed, with tunnel vision and laser focus toward that finish line. As adults, we need to pursue our goals and dreams with the same passion! On your mark, get ready, set…GO!

March 29th

People start moving as a result of either inspiration or desperation. Whichever one has motivated you doesn't matter. What matters is that you are moving. You are taking a step forward and coming closer to your dreams and goals. Seize the moment and maximize the opportunity!

March 30th

Ladies, just a word of advice from one woman to another: Go where you are *celebrated*, not *tolerated*!

March 31st

When life throws you curve balls, you have to make a decision: (1) Stand still and get hit; (2) Duck; (3) Step up to the plate and give it all you've got with the mightiest swing you can muster up. Then you go to the batting cage and practice. So when the next curve ball comes, you're ready for it.

APRIL

April 1st

This message is for all of my women friends, sistah-girls, women-preneurs, moms, girlfriends and wives: Stay encouraged. Oftentimes, *you* are the glue that holds it all together. We were designed with unimaginable strength (and I'm not talking about muscle mass) to be a bridge, the glue, the molding, the lifeline for our families and communities. I celebrate you all!

April 2nd

The funny thing about money and excuses is that you can't make both at the same time.

April 3rd

It's time to get off the sideline, cheering for everyone else. It's time for you to get in the game! Don't get me wrong, it's more than alright to cheer for others; but you can't spend so much time there that you forget to pursue your dreams. Help others, but remember to stay focused and stay the course with your vision too!

April 4th

If you try not, you have not. If you ask not, you have not. If you make excuses, you have not. If you fail to plan and prepare, you have not. Don't let 'have not' be your story. Plan, prepare, ask and execute!

April 5th

I have corporations in my belly. I'm giving birth to my vision. I'm breathing air into the lungs of my dreams and I'm going to enjoy watching my dream castles grow. I understand that they won't grow without dedication and hard work. I'm willing to invest and make the effort. After all, this is my future I'm talking about.

April 6th

It's time to sharpen the saw! Focus on surrounding yourself with people that will sharpen you, push, pull and drag you over the finish line. Surround yourself with people that have positive energy, that have been where you want to go, that can and will encourage you, support you, and give you a kick in the pants when needed.

April 7th

Leadership 101: When your words and actions match, people know they can trust you. Don't talk the talk if you are not prepared to walk the walk.

April 8th

I beg to differ! You do *not* need to see *The Wizard of Oz* to get some courage. You do *not* need to eat a can of spinach for strength. You do *not* need to wear a special ring to activate your super powers. You just need to believe in yourself! You already have everything that you need.

April 9th

You cannot afford to spend time, energy or effort on things or people that add no value to your life. If there is something or someone draining you, distracting you, holding you down or holding you back or continuously taking from you, spiritually or naturally, make a decision to take your life back. You owe it to yourself! Let go and get back on track!

April 10th

We have all made mistakes. We've all had to ask for forgiveness at some point in our lives. However, what strikes me as odd is how people ridicule and judge one another as if they have never made a mistake or error in judgment. Stop pointing fingers and learn to lend a hand. Don't tear people down; find ways to lift them up.

April 11th

Today, I wish for you abundance. I want you to have an abundance of energy, hope, love, success, positivity, creativity, courage and happiness.

April 12th

I was born to win, prepared to win, destined to win. I don't know how to quit. I don't know how to stop pursuing my dreams. I don't know how to stop encouraging others. I don't how to say I can't. I believe I can do anything and everything I set my mind toward.

April 13th

What you seek, you will find. If you seek happiness, love, prosperity, peace and people of like-mind, you will find it or it will find you. However, if you are attracted to drama, negativity, and foolishness that's exactly what you will find. Be careful of what you put in the universe; it's like a boomerang--it will return to you.

April 14th

Tomorrow is not promised. Live your life today! Pursue your dreams, walk out on faith, stop holding grudges, and tell that person that you love them today. You're not guaranteed to have an opportunity to do it tomorrow.

April 15th

I will give my best and my last. I will not lose. I will not conform to mediocrity. I will always push myself. I will not give up nor give in. I will soar. I will outlast. I will not stop. Period.

April 16th

I woke up this morning and I was so hungry! I had an apple from the tree of life, enjoyed the buffet of courage, discipline, character and strength. Then I had a sip from the river of success, followed by a heaping spoonful of love, peace and blessings for dessert. What a meal!

April 17th

I'm on a mission today! I am finding reasons and ways to smile. I'm finding reasons and ways to give thanks. I'm finding reasons and ways to be happy and make others happy. What about you?

April 18th

Take a look at most successful people (whatever you determine success to be) and you will notice that they all have winning, friendly, approachable, eager attitudes. Change your attitude and change your life.

April 19th

Today, let's measure the cost. What's the cost of you *not* pursuing your dreams? What's the cost of you *not* going back to school? What's the cost of you *not* asking for that raise or promotion? What is fear and procrastination costing you? Measure it and make a decision to make deposits that will yield positive results for your future.

April 20th

If you didn't already know, the human touch is very powerful! It heals, it energizes, it rejuvenates, it comforts, it soothes and it says, "I love you," without saying a word. Touch or hug someone today.

April 21st

Communication is key. Talk until you have an understanding. Don't assume that the person you are engaged with knows how you feel or what you are thinking. Also, please learn to *listen*. Don't just wait for the other person to stop talking so you can jump in. Listen!

April 22nd

When I was a child, my mom would have my brother and I recite affirmations every morning before leaving for school. We would say things like, "I am all that I believe I am. I am loving, caring, honest, considerate, focused, happy, peaceful, kind and trustworthy." Somehow, as an adult, I lost the daily ritual but the foundation was set. Affirm who you are and who you want to be, *daily*.

April 23rd

Most people carry around emotional baggage that causes them to react to certain people or situations. Anytime that you become highly emotional when listening to another person, check your emotions, especially if your reaction seems to be stronger than the situation warrants.

April 24th

My recipe for a good day:

1 cup of positivity

1 cup of encouragement

2 cups of focus

1/2 cup of no excuses

1/2 cup of love

A pinch of salt

That coupled with twenty push-ups and I'm good to go! Create your own recipe for a great day and stick to it.

April 25th

I am walking in it today! I'm walking in faith; walking in light; walking in love; walking in hope; walking into opportunity; walking into possibilities; walking into prosperity; walking into abundance; walking in my purpose. I hope I bump into you along the way, which means we're on the same path!

April 26th

I feel so alive! I'm happy, I'm focused, I have a vision, I'm planning my work and working my plan. I'm drawing positive energy into my circle and releasing negative energy and negative people. I love myself and therefore, I'm able to love others. I feel good! If your battery has run down, plug into mine and get a boost.

April 27th

Today, I'm focused on how I can be a better *me*! I'm not concerned with what Bob, Bill, Sue or Jane is doing or what they said. I'm focused on how I can grow, how I can challenge myself to be better, how I can inspire others, how I can be a resource to others and how I can add value. What are you focused on today?

April 28th

Always remember that you are responsible for your own happiness. No matter what happens or doesn't happen in your life, to be happy is a choice that you make. I choose happiness because it's a comfortable place for me. I like being there because the alternative is pretty scary! Make a choice, today!

April 29th

Don't take the easy way out. It's easy to give up. It's easy to walk away. It's easy to say, "I quit." What builds your character is to fight through and fight for your dreams. Winners don't quit!

April 30th

Today, let's focus on commitment. Are you committed to your growth by reading about something in your industry or field daily? Are you committed to helping others? Are you committed to your goals? Are you committed to your success? If you answered, "No" to any of these questions, what are you committed to? It may be time to make some adjustments. Challenge your excuses!

MAY

May 1st

When you live, sleep and breathe your passion, you will find your greatest success. If your 9-5 isn't your passion, discover what your passion is and then find a way to get paid to do it!

May 2nd

Did you know that pride is the number one reason why people are not teachable? Today, measure the cost. What has pride cost you?

May 3rd

Silence and meditation are two places most of us don't spend enough time visiting, but it's where you find the most clarity.

May 4th

Today, I want to give a shout out to all the naysayers and energy-suckers! You have inspired me to press harder; focus more; dream bigger dreams; encourage others; warn folks to stay away from you and your mentality; build multiple businesses; write a book; have my name on the big screen; travel the world; speak another language. Yes, you did that. Thank you for the inspiration.

May 5th

Even though my father told me I wouldn't graduate high school; even though I didn't grow up in the best of neighborhoods; even though I didn't have the finest of things as a child; even though the people around me were self-destructing; even though I didn't have a frame of reference of what it was like to make your dreams come true, look at me now! Never allow your past to cripple you or damage your self-esteem. Use your past as building blocks to your future.

May 6th

Imagine how much further ahead we would be in life, in love, in our careers if we had just listened to that inner voice! Everyone has that inner voice that serves to guide us and warn us, but we don't always listen to it. Today, make a conscious effort to listen to it; it's trying to tell you something.

May 7th

I need you to do me a favor. If you are holding on to a belief of lack or fear of failure, release it today! Your thinking is the *only* obstacle preventing you from achieving your dreams. Let it go! Walk in faith, walk in abundance and believe in yourself and your abilities.

May 8th

I'm focused on the future and what deposits I can make *now* that will yield positive results in the future of my businesses, my family, my relationship, my health, my community and our youth. Today, let's sow some seeds of love and positivity.

May 9th

I realize that I have been blessed beyond measure and I am so grateful. I walk in abundance. I am filled with life, love, laughter and happiness. As a matter of fact, love, gratitude, happiness and I have become best friends. We do everything together and they always have my back. Today, focus on all the things you have to be grateful for.

May 10th

Sometimes we become so comfortable with the garbage in our lives that we resist change. We resist enlightenment. We are afraid to shake it loose and cleanse ourselves from the dirt that we're covered in and have become accustomed to. Shake it loose! Hose yourself down and rinse the dirt off. You have so much to do! The mud is holding you back. Shake it loose!

May 11th

Your attitude has the ability to lift you up or tear you down. You choose.

May 12th

We live in an age where our youth know the *price* of everything, but don't know the *value* of anything. In an age where we kill time, waste time and are on borrowed time, we can't make time to sit and listen to our loved ones. We live in an age where we plan our vacations better than we plan our lives. What's wrong with this picture?

May 13th

When you're walking the road less traveled, you can expect that you will encounter some lions, tigers and bears along the way. The key is preparation! I expect them; therefore, they don't catch me off guard.

May 14th

To be a winner, you have to be willing to roll your sleeves up; get in the trenches; push harder; move faster; study longer; be stronger; have vision; be a team player; know your competition; be humble and most of all stay focused and stay the course! I'm a winner!

May 15th

I just don't know! I don't know how to quit. I don't know how to give up on my dreams. I don't know how to not be optimistic. I don't know how to stop pressing onward and upward. I don't know how to not be a positive influence. I don't know how to say, "I can't" and I realize is that some things just weren't meant for me to know.

May 16th

I admire children because they know no fear. They believe they can do and be everything. We can learn a lot from them.

May 17th

I woke up this morning with a fever! I am burning up and on absolute fire about my dreams, my goals, and my direction. I am determined to make it happen! Don't let your flame burn out. Ignite and go!

May 18th

Happiness is a choice! I choose to be happy. I choose to surround myself with people that are happy, as we feed off each other's energy. The quality of your life is determined by how you feel at any given moment; make a conscience choice to be happy!

May 19th

Don't go for the obvious. If someone is out of sorts or out of character with you, don't snap at them or become angry or defensive. Explore the cause rather than criticize the action. They may need some words of encouragement from you.

May 20th

Stop hitting the snooze button on your dreams! Get up, plant your feet, stretch and get busy! The time is now!

May 21st

I feel incredible today! I am in love with life! Every twist and turn, every lesson, every success, every challenge and every learning opportunity has made me love it more. Ahhhhh, life is good. Live it! Love it! Enjoy it!

May 22ⁿᵈ

So fear is in the left corner, wearing the red trunks. You are in the right corner, wearing blue trunks. Ding, ding! The bell rings. I need you to come out swinging! Stop running around the ring with fear. Go on and knock it out!

May 23ʳᵈ

The only person that has the ability to define me is *me*. The only person that can prevent me from achieving my goals is *me*. The only person that can determine how successful I can be is (you guessed it) ME! Don't let others define who you are or where you can go. You decide!

May 24ᵗʰ

Our minds are so powerful! Imagine how amazing we would be if we learned how to use them fully, minus the garbage that we put into them daily.

May 25th

It's time for you to take a look at those goals again. Where are you with your 3- or 6-month goals, 1-year goal, 5-year goal? Hold yourself accountable. Be realistic with your deadlines and stay focused and stay the course.

May 26th

I am *full* of it today! I am full of love, full of life, full of energy and I'm happy to share it with each of you!

May 27th

Let's be possibilitarians! Let's be solution developers! Let's be optimists! Let's be playmakers! Let's get in the game! Are you with me?

May 28th

When we were children, we would dream of what we wanted to be when we grew up, where we wanted to live, what we wanted to drive and who we wanted to marry. When we become adults, do we stop dreaming or do we start making our dreams a reality?

May 29th

I had to apologize to someone for yelling at them. I was angry with myself for allowing this person to push me to the point that I behaved out of character. Learn from my mistake; don't allow others to push your buttons. When you do, you give them the control.

May 30th

Food for thought: What comes out of your mouth is determined by what goes into your mind. Garbage in, garbage out. Positivity in, positivity out! Truth in, truth out!

May 31st

What kind of support system do you have? Who do you talk to when you need help or advice? If you don't have at least two close friends that you can confide in, without fear of ridicule or judgment, you really need to change your circle of friends!

JUNE

June 1st

Realize that as you grow and stretch in your thinking and living, your friends will change! Everyone will not grow at the same pace that you will. Some won't grow at all. Don't get stuck trying to hold on to past relationships that weigh you down. Cherish them and the memories, be grateful for the experience, then keep it moving and make new friends and expand your circle.

June 2nd

Some folks have a poverty mindset. They have a mindset of lack and struggle, of never having enough and just getting by. In order to change your conditions, you must change your thinking! Visualize abundance, prosperity and happiness, and put a plan in motion to get there.

June 3rd

If you believe you've done your very best, dig just a little bit deeper. If you believe you can't take one more step, dig just a little bit deeper. If you believe you have nothing left to give, dig just a little bit deeper. Keep digging. Just don't give up!

June 4th

Faith is what sustains you when all else fades or falls away. In your darkest hour when you are tired, when you are frustrated, when you are angry, when you are crying, when you feel no one has your back, when you're down to your very last, have faith that God has something in store for you and you will make it through. Your faith will be a testimony to others who have lost theirs.

June 5th

Do you have a plan? Stop complaining about what you don't like and develop a plan to have what you want, whether it's more money, happiness, a new job, a new house, a new car, peace of mind, a loving marriage, etc. Whatever you want, develop a plan to achieve it. Stay focused and stay the course.

June 6th

When you love someone, you don't judge; you don't criticize; you don't ridicule; you don't prosecute; you don't tear them down. Love encourages, motivates, inspires, supports, builds up and fights through! If someone claims that they love you and they tear you down, cut them hard and cut them fast! Love yourself enough to let them go!

June 7th

As children, we seek to please our parents, never wanting to see disappointment in their eyes. As adults, we strive to impress people that don't love us or have our best interests at heart. Stop trying to matter to people who don't matter. Who cares what they think?

June 8th

Are you a leader or a follower? As a child, my mom would always tell my brother and me to be leaders, not followers. As an adult, I realize all great leaders know how to follow, know when to follow, and know whom to follow!

June 9th

Communication is the key. Talk with (not to) your spouse. Talk with your children. Talk with your parents. Talk with your friends. Open up and share yourself with those you love. You won't regret it. You will develop a more meaningful relationship as a result.

June 10th

What will you do today to step up your game? I challenge you today to find three ways to take your business or personal relationships to the next level. Plan, prepare and then execute!

June 11th

You have to give people time to heal. If you've wronged someone, give them the opportunity to heal in their time, not in yours.

June 12th

Until you eat, live, sleep, drink and breathe your dream, you're just passing time. You can't realize your dream by wishing it into existence. You've got to put the work in.

June 13th

Let me share something with you that I have learned: you can't do it alone! You need help, I need help, and we all need help at some point in our lives. It may not be financial help either. Help comes in many forms. Don't be afraid to ask for help.

June 14th

It might be time for a detox in your life. Rid yourself of toxins that take shape in the form of toxic people, toxic habits, toxic jobs, toxic thinking and of course, toxic food. Develop a plan to rid yourself of the toxins today.

June 15th

Eliminate the words, "I can't" from your vocabulary and replace them with the words, "I will." We'll say them together. I will succeed, I will be happy, I will overcome, I will find a way or make a way, and I will not stop!

June 16th

Develop a sense of urgency. Develop a plan, a strategy that will bring you one step closer to your goals.

June 17th

You know, I won't allow myself to watch TV until I've completed something toward my goals every evening because I feel guilty sitting there, knowing I can't get that time back and I didn't use it wisely.

June 18th

I am convinced. I'm convinced that God created me with everything that I need, to be everything that I want. I'm convinced that every lesson learned along the path was to strengthen me and encourage me to keep pressing forward. I'm convinced that my job is to share my testimony with others. I'm convinced that with faith, determination, focus and love, I'm unstoppable!

June 19th

It feels good when you complete a task and you have a sense of accomplishment. I completed one of my goals today and I am celebrating! Then I'll spend some time updating my goals to reflect this accomplishment and what I plan to tackle next.

June 20th

I refuse to indulge in self-doubt or self-pity! God reminds me daily of just how blessed I am and I realize that I have an obligation to bless others.

June 21st

I don't know if there is anything more empowering than to know that someone believes in you! That is powerful! Today let someone else know that you believe in them!

June 22nd

I want you to give folks a time out today. Give a time out to anyone that is trying to steal your joy, steal your dreams, steal your happiness, steal your energy, steal your vision, or steal your peace. Put them in time out. Stay focused and stay the course.

June 23rd

Life is all about negotiations. You give a little, you take a little and you compromise. This is true not only in business, but in relationships in general. Never enter into a negotiation with a closed mind (my way or no way) or you have already failed.

June 24th

Do you have an accountability partner? Who do you share your dreams and goals with? Are they helping you to stay focused and stay the course? It's easy to be distracted by the grind of day-to-day life or other issues. Your accountability partner helps you stay on track and remain focused through completion of your goals. If you don't have one, please consider it. Their presence is invaluable

June 25th

I realize that I need to make some sacrifices in order to get to the other side; we all do.

June 26th

I have a question for you: What would you do if you weren't afraid? Would you pursue your degree, pursue your entrepreneurial dreams, learn a new language, travel overseas, change your eating habits, maybe ask for a raise? What would you do?

June 27th

I really believe I can do anything and everything that I want! I really believe that I don't have any limitations! What do you believe about yourself?

June 28th

Today is just the beginning! Walk out on faith, build with determination and aggressively pursue your dreams with laser-like focus!

June 29th

Everything is first a thought! Thoughts are powerful indeed. Today, be conscious of what you allow to enter your mind (via music, TV, or even other people). Is the information helping you to grow? If not, don't allow it to enter your mind!

June 30th

I want to know if you have allowed the naysayers to discourage or *motivate* you. Have you been a naysayer to someone else's dreams or visions? Has someone told you that you can't and therefore, you have told others that they can't? Inspire, motivate and encourage someone; you may be that spark of fire that they need so they won't give up!

JULY

July 1st

Did you realize that over 50% of your communication with others is conveyed via your body language? What is your body language saying?

July 2nd

I am in the business of helping others. There is no greater reward than helping others achieve their goals and their dreams. Become a resource, be a friend, be a leader, and be a blessing to someone else.

July 3rd

Networking is the single most effective tool used to advance a person's career, yet it's not being taught in schools. What will you do today to expand your network?

July 4th

There are those that *talk* and those that *do*. Make a decision to move away from the talkers and join the doers!

July 5th

When the window of opportunity closes, go open the door and walk through it!

July 6th

To quote my mom: "You'll get more flies with honey than you will with vinegar."

July 7th

I want to know who will you reach today, teach today, inspire today, hug today, motivate today, empower today, encourage today? Who?

July 8th

Today, no matter what challenges you face (no matter how big they seem), take a deep breath and say to yourself, "I've got this!"

July 9th

I am reflecting this evening on how grateful I am to be surrounded by angels that love me unconditionally; those angels disguise themselves as family and friends. I appreciate and value your presence in my life.

July 10th

I am allergic to drama and negativity. So, I surround myself with positive, goal-oriented people and you should, too.

July 11th

I am curious who took 15 minutes today to read something relative to your industry or business, whether online, in a book, or in a magazine. Please make a commitment to do something every day to sharpen your skills and your knowledge!

July 12th

I am growing and soaring to new heights, with no boundaries or limitations. Watch this eagle spread her wings.

July 13th

I wonder when you awakened this morning, did you visualize yourself having the day that you wanted to have? If not, it's not too late. Take five minutes right now to see yourself walking in greatness! Create the day that you want to have. Be exceptional today!

July 14th

Encourage someone to be a volunteer. Give your time, your heart and your expertise and make a difference! Make a positive impact! Be a blessing to others!

July 15th

Take charge of your attitude. Don't let someone else choose it for you! Be mindful of your attitude and remember that you have the ability to choose whether it's negative or positive! Expect a phenomenal day!

July 16th

I am building dream castles in the sky! They are limitless, boundless and reaching new heights! This is my story and the canvas is how I paint it.

July 17th

I realize that people are afflicted by various addictions. These addictions come in the forms of food, alcohol, women, men, and even drama. Yes, some people are addicted to drama. Take a look at your addictions and ask yourself if you've been able to positively benefit from them and if not, what will you do to break the habit?

July 18th

I am living, doing and enjoying this thing called life, busy planning my work *and* working my plan!

July 19th

"There's no such thing as coulda, shoulda, or woulda. If you shoulda and coulda, you woulda done it."

~ (Pat Riley)

I'm building a team of done it, did it, and doing it. Who's with me?

July 20th

We will either suffer the pain of discipline or the pain of regret. Which one will you choose? Which will yield the biggest reward for you?

July 21st

I am hot as a firecracker today! I'm on fire about what the future holds for me; I'm on fire about the lives that I want to impact positively; I'm on fire about what God has designed me to do. I'm on fire about the support of friends and family and I'm on fire because I'm inspired!

July 22nd

Don't make excuses, make changes. Change yields results. Excuses yield failure.

July 23rd

In 2004, I worked as a Sr. Recruiter for Quicken Loans/Rock Financial. One of QL's isms was, "Every client, every time. No exceptions. No excuses." That still resonates with me today as a business owner. Family, let's stop making excuses. Nail it down and get it done!

July 24th

There's something special about being able to recharge your battery by plugging in to those who love you and inspire you. Powerful fuel indeed! I am blessed and so grateful!

July 25th

I am putting the full court press on my goals! It's time to pound the boards!

July 26th

Make a conscious decision to *respond* and not *react*. Response is positive; reaction is negative. Don't allow anyone to control your emotions by pressing your buttons. You decide! Expect a phenomenal day!

July 27th

Sometimes we talk so much that we believe talking translates to action. It doesn't! Let's not talk about it, let's be about it! Are you with me?

July 28th

When you have passion, you're not focused on how many hours of sleep you didn't get. When you're living your dream, you're not concerned with what others think. When you're focused and determined, you will either find a way or *make* a way! I'm passionate about living my dream and I will make a way! What about you?

July 29th

I am bouncing back and forth from one leg to the other, one high heel to the other, practicing my right jab, with the theme from *Rocky* playing in the background. This fight will be a one-round KO!! Ding, ding! I'm coming out swinging! Procrastination just got knocked out!

July 30th

Some fail, while others succeed; some are sick, others are healthy; some are miserable, others happy. We all want to blame luck or fate or someone else, but the difference is within ourselves. We are the product of our habits and thoughts. Change your thinking and your conditions will change!

July 31ˢᵗ

What kind of seeds are you planting? What seeds were planted in you? Do you need to pull out the weed wacker?

AUGUST

August 1st

I am putting all energy-suckers (negative, pessimistic and draining people) on notice. Your time is up! If it's coming through the phone, I'm hanging up. If it's coming through the door, I'm locking the dead bolt. If it's coming through email, let me hit this delete key. Find something positive to talk about or stop talking to me.

August 2nd

The definition of insanity is doing the same thing over and over again, and expecting a different result. Today, make a commitment to break a bad habit. Make a commitment to form a new habit that will yield positive results for you.

August 3rd

I am spending time today reflecting on friendships. I've been so blessed over the years to establish, maintain and nurture some wonderful friendships.

August 4th

What's holding you back? What are you afraid of? Make up your mind to move, to execute, to stop procrastinating! Look fear in the eye and tell it this is it! You have no more control! Faith has taken over!

August 5th

I remember when my mom would to take my brother and me to the Vernors' plant on Woodward (tour and free samples). Every Wednesday we had dinner at Flaming Embers and once a month, she took us horseback riding. She is my hero!

August 6th

It's time to get uncomfortable with mediocrity! If you are comfortable with complacency and mediocrity, then it's time to stretch yourself, push yourself and take it to the next level! Decide to be uncomfortable and then do something about it.

August 7th

Do something extraordinary today! Be bold and courageous! What have you been on the fence about? Get excited about it today; go after it today; make it happen today; claim it today; own it today! I believe in you!

August 8th

Sometimes, the hardest thing for us to do is ask for help. You can't get the help you need if you never ask. Everyone that I know that has achieved *any* amount of success has had people in their corner that helped them in some way, shape or form.

August 9th

Happiness is not by chance; it's by choice. What decision will you make?

August 10th

Today, let's make an effort to find the positive in every situation that we encounter. Approximately 95% of your emotions are determined by how you interpret events. Make a decision to find the positive!

August 11th

I realize that there is something to be said for the man or woman that has the ability to be disciplined *and* focused! The fruits of their labor are in the achievement of their goals.

August 12th

I am reviewing my goals to measure my progress and to set new ones. Who's with me? If you don't have a clear plan for your life, you'll end up any and everywhere. Set obtainable goals.

August 13th

Another quote from my mom is, "I may have been born at night, but not last night." I heard this each and every time I tried to pull a fast one on her. We seem to forget that our parents were once teenagers, too.

August 14th

I want to know, are you going to cop out, hold out, drop out or go all out for your dreams? The decision is yours. What are you going to do?

August 15th

I have redefined my 'why' and my focus is even greater! What is your 'why'? What motivates you to go to work every day, to get out and make it happen every morning? Is it your children, your spouse, financial independence, notoriety? Examine your 'why' and determine if you are doing everything possible for it. If not, it's time to get busy.

August 16th

I found out that coulda, woulda and shoulda were left home alone. Courage, passion and make-it-happen were out hitting the streets and getting it done! Leave the excuses at home today. Nail it down and get it done!

August 17th

Oftentimes, we are our own worst critic. We are harder on ourselves than anyone else could possibly be. Today, take the time to pat yourself on the back and congratulate *yourself*! Job well done!

August 18th

I woke up this morning and had this crazy idea! I thought that I would decide to have a phenomenal day. I decided to have a productive day. I decided to have a positive mental attitude! Oh boy, me and my bright ideas! Hope they're contagious!

August 19th

I want you to get UNCOMFORTABLE TODAY! Introduce yourself to two perfect strangers (networking); make that phone call you've been putting off; forgive that person that angered you; set 3-, 6-, and 12-month goals for yourself; tell your spouse that you appreciate them; let your children know that you appreciate the love and laughter they have brought into your life.

August 20th

I realize that not everyone will be as positive, optimistic and upbeat as I am. However, if you're around me long enough, I will turn you to the bright side of the force! No Jedi mind tricks involved; only love and happiness.

August 21st

Not a pebble, not a stone, not even a hill. I feel like moving *mountains* today! Can't stop! Won't stop!

August 22nd

I'm sure we've all heard that people come into our lives for a reason, a season or a lifetime. Take a moment to reflect on those relationships and the lessons learned from them. And high five to the lifetimers!

August 23rd

I will be giving special attention and time to building the Tammy Turner brand today. Your personal brand is a key element to your success.

August 24th

I just spent time refining my 3-6 month goals, my one year goals and my 5 year goals. My vision and direction is crystal clear! I will keep my goals on me at all times in my wallet as a constant reminder. You should consider doing the same.

August 25th

I want you to share these three powerful words with someone: I appreciate you. When you say those three words, watch how you brighten their day (and yours).

August 26th

Today, I connected two individuals that I would not have otherwise met. This was a significant contact for one of the individuals. This is the power of networking! I gained absolutely nothing from the connection, other than the satisfaction of knowing that I was able to positively impact the life of another person. That's what I live for.

August 27th

There's someone close to you (family, friend, colleague) that needs your help. Reach out to them. They're ready to hear you. You won't regret extending a helping hand.

August 28th

I am experiencing the storm before the calm. You know that feeling you get when you *know* that you're on the right track, your vision is clear, you've seen yourself where you want to be, and the whole universe is conspiring to give you your heart's desire. Yes, that's where I'm at. It's uncomfortable at times and exhilarating at others.

August 29th

I realize that sometimes we are captivated by the sound of our own voice. We talk about what we're going to do for so long that we believe that equates to actually doing something. It doesn't!! We must graduate from talk to execution.

August 30th

Once you believe it, you internalize it, you see it, you plan for it, you step in it, and you expect it. You will achieve and obtain it. You are the only thing holding you back.

SEPTEMBER

September 1st

I am sending a shout out to all the strong men and women who are always STRONG for everyone that they love and whom oftentimes can't find anyone to be a pillar of strength for them. Sometimes we need a hug too, and I'm sending you one right now. (((hug)))

September 2nd

I want grown folks to stop believing in the boogeyman! Stop being afraid of the dark: afraid of the noise, or afraid of your own shadow. Cut on the lights. Face the fear that's holding you back.

September 3rd

I am learning to see God in everything and everyone. I see God in the flowers, the trees, my dog, my neighbor, the homeless and even the people that make me upset, which is sometimes the biggest challenge. I believe that when you *truly* see God in everything, you learn to embrace the difference and appreciate the beauty.

September 4th

There can be no growth without change. What and how are you willing to change in order to achieve the growth that you desire?

September 5th

I want you to eliminate the belief in lack (lack of love, lack of wealth, lack of time). I want you to see yourself living in abundance in these exact areas. Visualize it! Create a mental picture and position yourself to receive!

September 6th

Focus today on the power of allowing: allow love into your life; allow abundance into your life; allow wealth into your life; allow good health into your life. Allow no room for doubt in your life!

September 7th

When something bad happens, you have three choices: let it define you, let it destroy you, or let it strengthen you. The choice is yours.

September 8th

I realize that I am still on a journey of self-discovery. Sometimes I feel like I'm on date and I'm excited about the new things that I'm learning about my new friend.

September 9th

Can you help me spread the word? The word is: "Stop complaining!" Be a solution developer! If you are unhappy with something or someone, change it or make a decision to deal with it, but please stop complaining!

September 10th

I want you to know that what you're going through (and your breakthrough) is going to be a testimony to others! Don't give up! Don't quit! Stay the course!

September 11th

I'm focusing on forgiveness today. I have a couple of, "I forgive you" phone calls to make. I'm ready to move forward and no longer carry the hurt (or negative energy) with me. Do you have some calls to put in today? Make a commitment to make at least two of those calls today!

September 12th

You are the architect of your house and your destiny! Whether a house or a pyramid, the blueprint lies within. Dream, plan, build, and then dream, plan and build some more.

September 13th

You never know what storm a person is going through. You never know what trials and tribulations they've just overcome. We oftentimes are so quick to judge people, but couldn't walk a mile in their shoes. Let's practice kindness, love, patience and forgiveness with people. Your kind act or gesture could make the difference in their life.

September 14th

Give up on your need to always be right. You have to evaluate if it's more important to be right or to be happy.

September 15th

I married my husband because I trust his leadership; therefore, I happily submit to him as his wife and I don't question his judgment to lead me or our family. If I had doubts about his ability to lead, I would not have married him.

September 16th

I am proud to announce that I have given up on doubt. I gave fear the wrong number and I shut the door on "I can't." I choose to prosper and help others prosper. I choose to love and be loved. I choose to find a way or make a way because I can't stop and won't stop.

September 17th

There's no over-the-counter medication that I can take or prescription that I can fill that will help me with my allergic reaction to drama, negativity or energy-suckers. So, to avoid breaking out in hives or worse, I simply choose to avoid these types of people and the energy that they bring.

September 18th

I went to replenish my contact lenses yesterday and encountered a sales representative that had an unpleasant attitude and gave us the impression that she didn't want to help us. Now, we could have responded with an equally bad attitude, but we didn't. It was obvious that she was having a bad day. My husband and I instead attempted to cheer her up and encourage her. She provided us with what we needed and by the time we left, she thanked us for the encouraging words. You never know what someone is going through, so instead of reacting to a seemingly bad attitude, react with kindness. It may be the inspiration that the person needs to make it through their day.

September 19th

The dictionary is the only place where success comes before work! We've got some goals to achieve, so let's get to work. Get it in and get it done today! No excuses.

September 20th

Sometimes the hardest thing to do is look in the mirror and reflect on the image that you see. I'm not talking about the image looking back at you; I'm speaking of the image behind the eyes. It's always easiest to pick out the faults of others, but harder when it comes to seeing our own. Let's all take Michael's advice and, "Start with the Man in the Mirror."

September 21st

Goals have made a tremendous difference in my life. They have allowed me to achieve success and to accomplish what I had previously only dreamed of or wished for. Set goals!

September 22nd

Never let your memories become greater than your dreams! Sometimes, we get so stuck in the past that we forget to live in the present and prepare for the future.

September 23rd

Pursuing your dreams can be exhausting at times. But, imagine the feeling you will have when you're standing at the finish line. Begin with the end in mind.

September 24th

I am all that I believe I am! I am empowered; I am encouraged; I am intelligent; I am wise; I am happy; I am successful; I am inspired; I am humble; I am loving; I am grateful; I am peaceful and I am a winner! So are you!

September 25th

If the people that you believe are in your corner can't support you, encourage you, counsel you, cry with you or just listen to you, then it's time to reevaluate either them or what you believe it means to be in your corner.

September 26th

Ten years ago, I didn't know that I would start my own business. Five years ago, I didn't know I would write a book. One year ago, I didn't know I would meet, fall in love and marry the man of my dreams. But all those years ago and even today, I always had faith in my abilities and faith that God had wonderful things in store for me, even if at that given moment I didn't know who or what they were! Never lose faith!

September 27th

I am remembering the little things today and how they impact me and the lives of others. The little words like, "Please, thank you, good morning, hello, I'm sorry," or even a smile. Take some time today to remember the little things.

September 28th

It's time to get your grustle (grind + hustle) on and work toward achieving your goals. If you weren't happy with the progression of your goals last year, stay focused, be mindful of your thoughts, avoid negative people, and get an accountability partner. Let's make some forward progress!

September 29th

"Knowledge is power" is something I grew up hearing all of my life. Every time I heard it, I thought only of education as it related to school. As I get older, I think of it in different terms. Knowledge of self is power! In an attempt to gain power or exert power, we spend our lives focusing only on school education and we seem to lose sight of how important it is to master one's self. Now, please don't read this and think that I am minimizing the value of education, because I'm not. I'm only stating that in my humble opinion, there is nothing more powerful than a person that learns to master self (control of thought, control of action, and understanding how powerful your mind is). I'm learning something new about Tammy Turner every day and that knowledge empowers me!

September 30th

I am amazed at how easily some people give up. I'm not criticizing; I'm just amazed. You have to work hard toward whatever it is that you want. You have to visualize yourself where you want to be. You have to walk in faith. When you quit, you block your blessings! Don't block your blessings.

OCTOBER

October 1st

Courage is that place that you tap into when you feel like the world is against you. It's that place that you tap into when you feel like you have nowhere to turn. It's that place that you tap into when you feel like no one is in your corner. It's that place you tap into when you are discouraged, depressed or scared. Find the courage to keep moving forward. Find the courage to smile in the face adversity.

October 2nd

Achievement seems to be connected with action. Successful men and women keep moving. They make mistakes, but they don't quit. Quitters seem to develop a habit of quitting. Stay focused and stay the course.

October 3rd

Life's like a boomerang. The more good you throw out, the more you receive in return. However, the opposite is true. Today (and every day), let's practice kindness and patience. Let's throw as much good out there as we can and enjoy it when it returns to us.

October 4th

Excuses are well thought out lies. So stop using them and making them to justify not moving forward and pursuing your dreams. *You* are the only thing holding you back from the success you desire.

October 5th

Let go of the anger. Release it and forgive. Some of us have been holding on to anger for weeks, some for months and some for years. You're not hurting the other person; you're hurting yourself. Forgive them and keep it moving. Your health may depend on it.

October 6th

Our youth are counting on me and counting on you to blaze the trail for them. Let's lead by example. Let's walk in faith, not fear. Let's show our youth how great they can become when they follow their dreams and don't give up. It's up to us. Now, what are you going to do?

October 7th

Don't hit the snooze button on your dreams! The alarm is going off. It's time for you to hit the ground running and make it happen!

October 8th

It doesn't matter whether you're drinking Gatorade or Haterrade, you can't slow me down. Doesn't matter what you say or who you tell. Doesn't matter how loud you are or how sneaky you are. Doesn't matter whether you are trying to stand in my way or you are standing on the sideline. I will continue to excel! I will continue to push harder! I will continue to grow.

October 9th

I want you to pat yourself on the back. I want you to look at yourself in the mirror and say, "You're a winner." I want you to smile no matter what challenges you face today. Know that you are intelligent, wise, caring, powerful, successful, motivated and determined. Let's get it in and get it done today.

October 10th

If animals could talk, perhaps they could teach us how to stick together to accomplish a common goal. Perhaps they could tell us how to get creative instead of giving up. Perhaps they could show us how to share. Perhaps they could teach us how to trust our instincts. If animals could talk, maybe there's a lot we could learn.

October 11th

The Golden Rule: Do unto others as you would have them do unto you. There is no clause in that statement that says, "Except when you're having a bad day." Even when you're having a bad day, you still need to treat people with the respect that you desire.

October 12th

Somewhere, somehow, values and "rites of passage" that were once passed down from generation to generation have been lost. Women once taught their daughters how to be ladies and how to be wives. Men once taught their sons how to be gentlemen and husbands. When I look at our youth today, it's apparent that somewhere, somehow we dropped the baton instead of passing it on.

October 13th

Be focused, be bold, be courageous and meet challenges with confidence and optimism. Don't be distracted today. Stay focused and stay the course!

October 14th

How far are you willing to go to realize your dreams? Are you willing to fight through being tired? Are you willing to fight through being frustrated? Are you willing to fight through being disappointed? Are you willing to fight through being pushed down or dragged down? Chances are that you will encounter all of these things in your pursuit of your dreams. Fight through it! You'll be glad that you did.

October 15th

Do you remember when you were a child and you stood on your tippy toes to get that box of cereal out of the cabinet? Or you got a chair to reach those cookies on top of the refrigerator? As a child, your instincts said, "If I can't reach it, let me find or make a way." As adults, we forgot how to reach. We seem to expect the cereal to fall out of the cabinet and jump in a bowl for us. Or we expect the cookies (our dreams and goals) to fly off the top of the refrigerator and jump into a glass of milk and wait on the table for us to come and eat them. We have to allow those instincts to guide us in reaching our dreams and goals. I want you to stand on your tippy toes. I want you to reach and stretch yourself. Go after your dreams. Success is not going to be walking down the street one day and trip you or jump in your lap. You have to make it happen!

October 16th

Sometimes we are our own worst enemy. We spend so much time beating ourselves up over a bad decision we made, a missed opportunity, a failed relationship, money we lost, or a friendship we lost. Those challenging times happened for a reason. Stop beating yourself up! What did you learn about that bad decision? What did you learn about that missed opportunity (next time, seize the moment)? What did you learn after that failed relationship (about yourself and the other person)? What did you learn about the money you lost? What did you learn about the friendship you lost? These were all life lessons. You had to go through it to be who you are and where you are today. Don't regret it. Stop beating yourself up! Get the lesson, so you don't have to repeat it.

October 17th

You know we will make up an excuse for just about anything. We make excuses for why we can't make it to the gym, why we can't start that new business, why we can't go back to school, why we can't forgive, why we can't trust, why we can't just get started on whatever it is you keep telling yourself you're gonna do next week. It's time to challenge your excuses. Whatever it is that you are trying to do and whatever excuses that are holding you back, put a stop to it today!

October 18th

Attention! Severe happiness alert! I am predicting a day filled with abundance, filled with peace, filled with focus, filled with happiness, filled with love, filled with determination, filled with energy, filled with optimism. That's something the weatherman couldn't tell me (I got it from a higher authority)!

October 19th

"As a man thinketh, so shall he become." Be very conscious of your thoughts. Avoid negative thinking. Be careful of what you allow your mind to absorb, whether from TV, music, images or people. If you are feeding your mind positive, you will yield positive results. Expect a phenomenal week!

October 20th

I woke up hungry this morning. My breakfast options were: wisdom, determination, strength, love, courage, inspiration, motivation or vision. No matter what I pick, all of my options are healthy. There's nothing is like starting your morning off with a healthy breakfast.

October 21st

My happiness isn't dependent upon John, Sue, Jane, Jerome or Tom. My happiness isn't dependent upon if the weather is good or not. My happiness isn't dependent upon whether you're nice to me or if you had your coffee this morning. My happiness isn't even dependent upon how much money is in my savings account (although that contributes to my happiness). My happiness is dependent upon *me* and how good I feel about myself. Every time I stand behind a podium or in front of a room full of people and I'm able to inspire them, I know that I am walking in my purpose. That's where my happiness is derived from-- knowing who I am, knowing my purpose and walking in it.

October 22nd

Letting go can be healthy. Know when to embrace it.

October 23rd

I've come too far, I've struggled through too much, I cried too many tears, I stayed awake too many nights, I made too many changes, I asked God for guidance too many times--to be where I am right now, and then to give up. I'm not a quitter! I'm a fighter. I'm equipped with everything God has deposited within me. I got what I asked for: strength, guidance, wisdom and courage. So bring it on. Nothing will stop my stride; nothing is gonna slow me down.

October 24th

Twenty years from now, you will be more disappointed by the things you didn't do than by the ones you did do. So dream big, plan your work and work your plan. Don't live in fear. You can do it!

October 25th

Never act on emotion without the benefit of intellect. When you make a decision, whether personal or professional, that is based primarily on emotions, you tend to make bad choices that are difficult to recover from. So, take a step back, breathe, and think things through and make a decision based on intellect.

October 26th

People tend to make a change in their lives for one of two reasons: either inspiration or desperation. Whichever one is motivating you doesn't matter; embrace it and keep it moving. Change is inevitable.

October 27th

Today, I want you to either find a way or make a way! You can do it!

October 28th

If you are hanging around nine broke people, chances are pretty high that you'll be the tenth! Surround yourself with like-minded progressive people, people that inspire you and energize you when you get tired. Avoid folks that have no vision or their only goal in life is to steal your joy.

October 29th

Challenge yourself today! Do something different. Stop procrastinating. Be open to change and new ideas. Speak into existence that which you desire. Ask for help if you need it. Don't accept mediocrity. Know that you are everything that you believe you are! Do you accept your mission? This message will self-destruct in one day. So get busy!

October 30th

Sometimes people want the glory without the story. Good relationships are not just lying on the side of the road where you can pick them up, put them in your pocket and make them your own. Good relationships require work, commitment, dedication, love, respect, trust and vision.

October 31ˢᵗ

How many decisions have you made based on emotions such as pride, anger, ego, hurt feelings, jealously or animosity? Try making decisions based on intellect. Detach yourself from the emotion and you will make better decisions.

NOVEMBER

November 1st

It's time to get rid of that poverty mindset and belief in lack whether it's lack of finances, lack of resources or lack of love. Change your belief from lack to abundance. See yourself where you want to be. I see my future and it's so bright that I need to put on sunglasses to look at it!

November 2nd

If you really want to do something, you'll find a way. If you really don't, you'll find an excuse! Excuses lead to mediocrity. Mediocrity leads to failure. So, stop making excuses.

November 3rd

Pride can be very expensive! It can cost you happiness; it can cost you money; it can cost you peace of mind; it can even cost you relationships. Today, calculate how much pride has cost you and ask yourself was it worth the price you paid?

November 4th

Your attitude will determine your altitude. Stop walking around angry all the time! We all have bad days, but it's not okay to infect everyone else around you. Shake it off. Shake it loose. Choose to make it a great day!

November 5th

I've learned that you can't put a price tag on peace of mind. Its value is priceless!

November 6th

Surround yourself with people who love and support you. Walk with people who make you laugh, people who won't judge your tears and people that will weather the storm with you. Seek people that encourage, motivate and inspire you to be the best you possibly can. Avoid the energy-suckers at all cost.

November 7ᵗʰ

I believe there is someone for everyone. There is someone that God fashioned on the Potter's Wheel just for you. Not everyone will understand your love or your connection, and it's not important that they do. When you find that someone that was created just for you, let them know just how special they are and what their presence in your life means to you. Never take love for granted.

November 8ᵗʰ

The happiest people don't have the best of everything; they just make the best of everything. So, no matter what curve balls come your way (human, emotional, spiritual or physical), brush it off and keep smiling!

November 9ᵗʰ

I woke up today with this aching in my bones. It wasn't arthritis though. It was success! So, I rubbed on some determination and took a shot of focus. Now, I'm ready.

November 10th

I'm expecting a phenomenal day and I won't accept anything less! Mediocrity will not find a home here!

November 11th

The next time you're stressed, take a step back, inhale and laugh. Remember who you are and why you're here. You're never given anything in this world that you can't handle. Be strong, be flexible, love yourself and love others. Always remember, just keep moving forward.

November 12th

Hit the refresh button instead of snooze. Hit the refresh button on your dreams. Refresh your goals. Refresh your relationships. Refresh your ideas. Refresh your business or career. When you snooze, you lose. Refresh!

November 13th

If your get-up-and-go mentality has gotten up and left, plug into someone else's battery and get a boost. Just get going!

November 14th

Make a decision to get started today! Stop making excuses. Stop talking yourself out of it. Stop looking for validation from everyone else. Make up your mind and make it happen!

November 15th

The cut of the knife can heal, but the cut of the tongue lasts forever. Choose your words wisely and be mindful of how you talk to people, especially loved ones, especially when you're angry.

November 16th

I want to know what kind of mental food you had today. Was it nutritious? Or was it junk food?

November 17th

There are those that *make* things happen, those that *watch* things happen and those that *wonder* what happened. Don't find yourself wondering what happened. You're at the steering wheel; now drive the car.

November 18th

As the weather turns colder and you begin to pull those fall clothes out of storage, think about how the seasons in your life changed and you put your dreams in storage. It's time to retrieve them, blow the dust off, shine them up and get them ready for the fall. Get it in and get it done!

November 19th

One of the most deadly diseases today is an illness called jealousy. Folks today call it hating. Instead of hating on someone, find out what you can learn from them, how you can be better and do better. Knowledge and a good attitude is the cure. If someone has something or has achieved something that I desire, I see it as an opportunity to learn and I ask them to help me or show me how to get there. Knowledge is power! Don't be too prideful to ask for help. Those who ask not, have not.

November 20th

Be careful not to confuse movement with progress. A rocking horse moves, yet it makes no progress.

November 21st

You can't make the same mistake twice. The second time you make it, it's a choice.

November 22nd

We accept the love we think we deserve. If you *know* that you deserve more, then stop short changing yourself and accepting less than you deserve.

November 23rd

Never treat your dreams like they're a distraction to your busy schedule. That's the road to regret.

November 24th

How many times do you need to say, "Ouch"? Stop bumping your head on the same low ceiling: next time, duck. The moral of the story is stop repeating lessons that you should have already learned.

November 25th

They say that every day, a star is born. I say you are the star and you have the ability to be reborn and reinvent yourself whenever and however you choose. It starts with a strong belief in yourself and your abilities!

November 26th

Please understand that there are forces at work to destroy everything that you have worked hard to build; your character, your successes, your friendships and your relationships. If you give those forces energy by feeding into them, you will lose everything.

November 27th

I've learned that two people can look at the exact same thing and see something totally different.

November 28th

Where are all my winners at? I make a conscious choice to surround myself with winners, doers, believers, faith-walkers and faith-speakers. So, energy-suckers, Debbie-downers and pity-partiers, BEWARE. Your membership has been cancelled. Choose your circle wisely.

November 29th

I woke up today feeling like I should be doing more, so back to the basics. Decide what you want to do and then plan, prepare and execute. Be careful not to become complacent.

November 30th

If we listen to that little voice inside of us (some call it intuition) a little more often, we would probably be much further ahead in life, in love, and in our careers. Today, be conscious of what your intuition is trying to tell you.

DECEMBER

December 1st

Giving up is easy to do. The challenge is being able to fight through whatever it is that is preventing you from reaching your goal. You have what it takes. Stay focused and keep your mind on the end result.

December 2nd

No matter what your expertise, there's always room to grow and learn. The moment that you feel that you know everything is the moment that you stop growing.

December 3rd

Reality TV has made everyone desire to become famous. If you want to be known for something, be known as a person of integrity; be known as a person who is respectful; be known as a person of your word; be known as a person who gives; be known as a person who listens; be known as a person who loves; be known as a person who takes care of business; be known as a person who is honest. Now, that's something to strive for.

December 4th

Procrastination is the biggest destroyer of dreams. Make a conscious decision to stop procrastinating and get your dreams off the ground.

December 5th

When you love someone, it's not enough to just say it. You need to show it in your actions, in your smile, in your ability to put their needs above your own. Love is an action word.

December 6th

Our expectations are oftentimes the road to our disappointments. We expect someone to be kind, we expect someone to say, "Thank you," and we expect someone to know when or how to be there. Understand what your expectations are and realize that the only behavior that you can control is your own. When you expect people to do certain things, you set yourself up for a series of disappointments.

December 7th

Never ruin an apology with an excuse.

December 8th

Stop crying over people that are not worthy of your tears, your love, your heart, your time or your energy. That effort could be better spent on someone that wouldn't make you cry.

December 9th

When I was a child, my mom told me that, "Beauty was in the eye of the beholder." It took years for me to realize that I was the beholder. It was important for me to feel beautiful inside.

December 10th

Practice doesn't make perfect. Practice makes permanent. Take care when choosing what things you practice.

December 11th

Positive thinking is strong medicine for any ailment. Your thoughts can strengthen you or destroy you. The decision is yours.

December 12th

It's important to have dreams. Dreams are the road to success. However, those dreams must be accompanied by action. It takes action to make dreams come true.

December 13th

Whatever it is that you are going through right this moment, fight through it. You can do it. You have everything that you need to make it to the other side.

December 14th

Sometimes, it's uncomfortable to make the right decision. However, calculate how much it will cost you to make the wrong decision and you will see that in the end, the benefit outweighs the cost.

December 15th

Every time you encounter a challenge or an obstacle, it's a learning experience. These are character-building moments. Learn from the experience and it will make you stronger and equip you with the experience needed to help others.

December 16th

Discipline is not a bad thing. Discipline helps you to realize dreams and goals. Discipline is what stands between you and your ability to make your dreams a reality.

December 17th

Don't be afraid of change. Everyone must evolve. When you embrace change, it takes the fear away.

December 18th

The Law of Attraction (or simply put, karma) is strong and real. That which you put in the universe will be what is returned unto you. When you treat people with respect, love, honesty and a good attitude: that's the karma that you will receive. However, the opposite is also true.

December 19th

Leaders lead by example. They either show you the way or show you how to make a way.

December 20th

"I'm sorry" seems to be the two most difficult words in the English language, yet they bridge the most gaps, relieve the most pressure, and alleviate the most stress.

December 21st

Your finances won't grow if your thinking doesn't. These go hand-in-hand. When you begin to stretch your mind and your thinking, your finances will follow.

December 22nd

If you go through life blaming others for your failures, you will continue to fail. When you take responsibility for your failures and learn from your mistakes and bad choices, you are on the road to realizing your dreams.

December 23rd

In order to go up, you have to get up. You have to get fired up. You have to wake up and make up for lost time.

December 24th

I've heard that if you do something for 21 days, it becomes a habit. Well, let's practice positive thinking for 21 days and develop a new habit.

December 25th

Whether you choose to celebrate Christmas or not, take time on this day to celebrate and enjoy family. Christmas isn't about how many material gifts you give or receive; it's about the gift of love that you share with your family and loved ones.

December 26th

When you love someone, you don't put love in a measuring cup and only give a certain amount on a certain day; your cup should be running over.

December 27th

I don't spend time identifying other people's faults. I have enough character flaws of my own to work on.

December 28th

Find something that you love to do, then find a way to get paid to do it. That's the definition of success.

December 29th

Nothing can make or break you without your permission.

December 30th

When you start to lose focus and begin to procrastinate, think about how good it felt the last time you completed a task that you set out to do. You remember the sense of accomplishment that you felt? Let that feeling be your motivation to get going and get it into gear.

December 31st

I remain confused as to why people make New Year's resolutions. Why do you need to wait until the beginning of a new year to decide to make changes in your life and/or break bad habits? If there is something in your life that you want to change, do it now! Why wait?

ABOUT THE AUTHOR

Tammy is a recruiter, author, public speaker and Trainer. Tammy is the owner of Kapstone Training Services, LLC and Kapstone Publishing. Tammy is also an Engineering Recruiter with Diversified Services.

After serving for over six years in the field of public accounting, having worked at major firms such as Arthur Andersen and Deloitte & Touche, Tammy realized that her true passion was in the field of Human Resources. More specifically, she wanted to personally help place people in various positions of employment. As such, Tammy worked as a recruiter for Robert Half Finance & Accounting and a senior recruiter at Quicken Loans/Rock Financial. In 2004, Tammy was able to travel overseas to Cambodia, where she worked at the International School of Phnom Penh (ISPP) and as a recruiting consultant for UNICEF and HR, Inc. Cambodia. Tammy returned to the United States in 2007 and pursued her entrepreneurial dreams and established Kapstone Training Services and in 2010 she established Kapstone Publishing.

Tammy's "Elements of Success" program has helped shape the careers of students and business professionals throughout the U.S. and abroad. In this program, she offers training on executive presence, business etiquette and image, dining etiquette, interviewing tips, and skills to successfully master the art of networking. Her debut book, *How to Talk to Strangers: A Step-by-Step Guide to Professional Networking*, is a vital tool for any business professional looking to go to the next level. Your mother may have told you not to talk to strangers, but Tammy teaches you how to talk to them. Tammy's second book, 365 Days of Motivation: A Guide to Success in Life & Business is a must have for anyone and everyone looking for encouragement or inspiration in their daily business or personal relationships.

Tammy has served on the Board of Directors of various organizations such as NABA (National Association of Black Accountants), SAFE (Sisters Acquiring Financial Empowerment) and The Web Academy. Tammy is a wife and a mother. Tammy enjoys watching football, skiing and is an avid golfer.

www.ingramcontent.com/pod-product-compliance
Lightning Source LLC
Chambersburg PA
CBHW050827160426
43192CB00010B/1932